LINGERING THOUGHTS

PRIYANKA GURUNG

Copyright © Priyanka Gurung
All Rights Reserved.

This book has been published with all efforts taken to make the material error-free after the consent of the author. However, the author and the publisher do not assume and hereby disclaim any liability to any party for any loss, damage, or disruption caused by errors or omissions, whether such errors or omissions result from negligence, accident, or any other cause.

While every effort has been made to avoid any mistake or omission, this publication is being sold on the condition and understanding that neither the author nor the publishers or printers would be liable in any manner to any person by reason of any mistake or omission in this publication or for any action taken or omitted to be taken or advice rendered or accepted on the basis of this work. For any defect in printing or binding the publishers will be liable only to replace the defective copy by another copy of this work then available.

Dedicated to generation
Just like mine
who seek for a peaceful mind.

Contents

Foreword

MRK Publications Office: Sainkpuri, TCP More(Khaprail Bazar), Siliguri, Darjeeling(W.B)-734009Contact: 8116782587, email- ranjanthapa316@gmail.com

Preface

Hi, I'm Priyanka Gurung. I write poetries and quotes based on life experiences. My poetries are about expression and thoughts. It's more like creating a comfortable space in mind. My poetries are about cherishing moments, about hard times, about peaceful environment, and about unsaid worries.

1. it just smiled back

I pondered how lucky the couples'
were as somebody was along their side.
Saw my own reflection and
it just smiled back,
as I knew my Romeo
never left my side.

2. Mind lies a distinct creature.

Only the Mind knows the agony of unstable state and
unplanned future.
The lips says it's fine but only the mind knows the hazy
picture.
This fragile mind being judged and eyed on, gets tangled in
its own ideas.
Once which was confident is now petrified,
scared to make any mistake as thoughts and
words repeats on its own leaving it baffled.
Engulfed in all these uproar of Unset
Mind lies a distinct creature.

3. Again

Again
I wish I was a kid again,
And wonder on the road with my friends again.
Would roll on the ground,
And run on the fields.
Would get chased by the sun and wind,
Dripping sweat and huffing breath,
Laughter is caught in the air.
Without worrying about anything else,
Would enjoy my life all over again.

4. Into the blue land

Into the blue land, I dive deeper and deeper.
Being swallowed by the charismatic world.
That makes my heart beat fast.
So fast until it starts to burn me up.
My lungs starts to gasp for air,
But the air is found no where.
I start to turn blue like the blue land,
So I struggle to escape from this land.
Only to get clenched by it, again and again.
Now all I have left is a numb feeling and a cold heart.
And slowly I start to drift apart,
Apart from the world and the sunlight,
Now all I know is that,
I wanna wish myself a good night.

5. With that the lost Touch. Found.

Scrolling through my phone a text comes to light,
filling my heart with a familiar warmth.
Old memories, reminiscence inside my mind.
Forming curves on my lips,
and creating folds near my eyes.
Finger hastily tap on the text;
Which reads "Hey! it's been a while"
and with that the lost Touch. Found.

6. Tell me your experience

Tell me your experience,
I'll tell you mine.
Tell me your pain,
I'll tell you mine.
Show me your worries,
I'll try to understand it.
Will always try to make you feel at ease.
Share your thoughts,
I won't judge you.
If you are looking for a comfort zone,
I'll be the one for you.
Cause I'll be here for you.

7. "Peace is still here in chaos."

Sitting on the last bench and listening to the hustle of the
class,
barely conversing with any soul, rather wondering in my own
world.
Looking around and paying attention to every details
from their laugh to their small gossips,
from the sound of the ceiling fan to their feet tapping,
from their scribbling notes to them grooving to music.
Bringing smile on my face and pleasing my ears,
all I think is "Peace is still here in chaos."

8. But still beautiful

You look like her.
Gave her mixed feeling.
Similar faces,
Similar personality.
And there is the similar smile,
Cause she was happy.
Because she looked like the one,
She had admired all her life.
Who now has wrinkles,
And grey hair.
But still beautiful,
As if she never aged.

9. He/Him

He/Him

She said you can be the way you want.

They said no, You should be manly.

She said it's okay to be different.

They said be like a man.

She said listen to your heart.

They said society decides.

She said you are looking beautiful in that dress.

They said you look feminine, it's not what men wears.

10. She/Her

She/Her

He said you can do it.

They said you were not meant for it.

He said laugh out loud.

They said you are not supposed to be loud.

He said it's your life, your choice.

They said your life is already decided.

He said it's okay to be masculine.

They said behave, behave like a lady.

List Of Books Under Mrk Publications

1. Problem Solving through 'C' Programming- Aslam J. Karjagi

2. MIL Hindi (NBU New Syllabus)- Ashis Thakur

3. Manaka Kathaharu- Mandira lepcha

4. Life Changing Thouhts- Ranjan Kumar Thapa

5. Solace- Shampa Mukherjee

6. Fairy Dust- Mayuri Churiwal

Available on Flipkart and Amzaon and MRK Store(Special Discount)

Contact us soon.